It's All the Same to Me!

Here's how to multiply or divide to get fractions of equal value.
These fractions are called **equivalent fractions**.

Different fractions can name the same number.

$$\frac{3}{4}\frac{(\times 4)}{(\times 4)} = \frac{12}{16} \qquad \frac{2}{4}\frac{(\div 2)}{(\div 2)} = \frac{1}{2}$$

Match equivalent fractions.

1. $\frac{2}{4}$ jar of pickles

$\frac{1}{3}$ jar

$\frac{1}{8}$ jar

$\frac{1}{2}$ jar

2. $\frac{5}{6}$ gallon of juice

$\frac{15}{18}$ gallon

$\frac{5}{12}$ gallon

$\frac{10}{20}$ gallon

3. $\frac{4}{5}$ loaf of bread

$\frac{8}{9}$ loaf

$\frac{16}{20}$ loaf

$\frac{7}{10}$ loaf

4. $\frac{3}{9}$ bag of cookies

$\frac{2}{4}$ bag

$\frac{2}{7}$ bag

$\frac{1}{3}$ bag

5. $\frac{12}{16}$ pizza pie

$\frac{3}{4}$ pie

$\frac{2}{3}$ pie

$\frac{1}{2}$ pie

6. $\frac{3}{8}$ c

$\frac{4}{10}$ cup

$\frac{6}{16}$ cup

$\frac{1}{4}$ cup

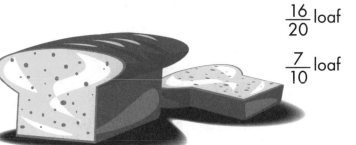

D1378977

Skill: Recognizing equivalent fractions

FRACTION IDEAS

An Easy Way to Reduce

Here's how to **reduce** a fraction **to lowest terms.** Divide the numerator and denominator by the **greatest common factor (GCF).**

 The GCF is the greatest number that divides each of the two numbers—the numerator and the denominator.

$$\frac{9}{12}\frac{(\div 3)}{(\div 3)}=\frac{3}{4}$$

Reduce each fraction to lowest terms.

1. $\frac{4}{6}\frac{(\div 2)}{(\div 2)}=\frac{2}{3}$

2. $\frac{6}{10}$ = _____

3. $\frac{3}{9}$ = _____

4. $\frac{5}{20}$ = _____

5. $\frac{4}{8}$ = _____

6. $\frac{12}{18}$ = _____

7. $\frac{14}{35}$ = _____

8. $\frac{10}{50}$ = _____

9. $\frac{8}{20}$ = _____

10. $\frac{9}{36}$ = _____

11. $\frac{22}{33}$ = _____

12. $\frac{300}{400}$ = _____

Skill: Reducing fractions to lowest terms

It's Not Improper Any More

A fraction is called an **improper fraction** if its top number (**numerator**) is equal to or bigger than its bottom number (**denominator**). Here's how to change improper fractions to whole numbers and mixed numbers. Divide the numerator by the denominator.

You can always write an improper fraction another way.

$$\frac{20}{4} \qquad 4\overline{)20} \atop \underline{-20} \atop 0 \qquad \frac{22}{6} \qquad 6\overline{)22} \atop \underline{-18} \atop 4$$

$$4\overline{)20} \quad \frac{5}{}$$

$$6\overline{)22} \quad 3R4$$

4 Remainder

$$\frac{20}{4} = 5 \qquad\qquad \frac{22}{6} = 3\frac{4}{6} = 3\frac{2}{3} \text{ lowest terms.}$$

Write each improper fraction as a whole number or as a mixed number in lowest terms.

1. $\frac{3}{2} = 1\frac{1}{2}$ **2.** $\frac{5}{5} =$ _____   **3.** $\frac{7}{4} =$ _____

4. $\frac{11}{10} =$ _____   **5.** $\frac{16}{3} =$ _____   **6.** $\frac{21}{7} =$ _____

7. $\frac{17}{8} =$ _____   **8.** $\frac{55}{6} =$ _____   **9.** $\frac{14}{4} =$ _____

10. $\frac{36}{9} =$ _____   **11.** $\frac{48}{12} =$ _____   **12.** $\frac{18}{10} =$ _____

13. $\frac{37}{7} =$ _____   **14.** $\frac{44}{20} =$ _____   **15.** $\frac{7}{1} =$ _____

Skill: Writing improper fractions as mixed or whole numbers

Fraction Action

Use what you know about fractions and mixed numbers to answer each question.

Don't forget to reduce to lowest terms.

1. Sue and Drew both had the flu. Sue drank $\frac{2}{8}$ of a quart of orange juice. Drew drank $\frac{4}{16}$ of a quart of orange juice.

Who drank more juice? **They drank the same.**

$$\frac{2}{8} \frac{(\div 2)}{(\div 2)} = \frac{1}{4} \qquad \frac{4}{16} \frac{(\div 4)}{(\div 4)} = \frac{1}{4}$$

2. Drake and Jake shared a cake. Drake ate $\frac{3}{6}$ of it, and Jake ate $\frac{5}{10}$ of it. Who ate more? _____

3. Bo and Joe watched it snow. Bo said the snow was $\frac{9}{12}$ of a foot deep. Joe said the snow was $\frac{3}{4}$ of a foot deep. Can they both be right? _____ Which fraction can you reduce? _____

4. Anita and Rita wrapped some cookies in boxes that held 6 cookies each. They filled $3\frac{2}{6}$ boxes. How many cookies was that? _____

5. Rudy and Judy made bracelets using glass beads. Judy's bracelet was $9\frac{1}{2}$ inches long. Rudy's was made of 20 half-inch beads. Whose was longer? _____

6. Glenn and Ben raised some hens. Glenn had $3\frac{1}{2}$ dozen eggs. Ben had $\frac{40}{12}$ dozen eggs. Who had more eggs? _____

Skill: Problem solving using fractions and mixed numbers

Workout!

Test Your Skill

Write the fraction or mixed number that each picture shows.

1.

2.

3.

4.

_____   _____   _____   _____

Write three different fractions with equal values for each fraction below.

5. $\frac{1}{2}$ = _____ = _____ = _____

6. $\frac{8}{12}$ = _____ = _____ = _____

Reduce each fraction to lowest terms.

7. $\frac{6}{24}$ _____

8. $\frac{12}{16}$ _____

9. $\frac{5}{15}$ _____

Write each as a fraction, whole number, or mixed number.
Make sure your answer is in lowest terms.

10. $\frac{8}{2}$ _____

11. $\frac{16}{3}$ _____

12. $\frac{6}{18}$ _____

13. $\frac{12}{9}$ _____

14. $\frac{18}{27}$ _____

15. $\frac{30}{6}$ _____

16. $\frac{17}{4}$ _____

17. $\frac{3}{4}$ _____

18. $\frac{25}{15}$ _____

Common Ground

Here's how to **add fractions** with **like denominators.**
Add **the numerators.** Write the sum over the denominator.

Be sure to write your answers
in lowest terms.

$$\frac{3}{5} + \frac{1}{5} = \frac{4}{5}$$

Find the sums. Give your answers in lowest terms.

1. $\frac{3}{8} + \frac{1}{8} = \frac{4}{8}$ $\frac{4}{8} \frac{(\div 4)}{(\div 4)} = \frac{1}{2}$

2. $\frac{3}{7} + \frac{2}{7} =$

3. $\frac{1}{3} + \frac{1}{3} =$

4. $\frac{5}{10} + \frac{3}{10} =$

5. $\frac{1}{4} + \frac{3}{4} =$

6. $\frac{3}{5} + \frac{4}{5} =$

7. $\frac{7}{9} + \frac{8}{9} =$

8. $\frac{3}{6} + \frac{4}{6} =$

9. $\frac{5}{12} + \frac{5}{12} =$

10. $\frac{9}{20} + \frac{11}{20} =$

Skill: Adding fractions with like denominators

It's All Mixed Up

Here's how to **add mixed numbers** with **like denominators**. Add the fractions. Then add the whole numbers. Simplify if needed.

Be sure to add the whole number parts together. Rename $9 + \frac{6}{5}$ as $10\frac{1}{5}$.

$$6\frac{4}{5}$$
$$+\ 3\frac{2}{5}$$
$$\overline{\quad\frac{6}{5}\quad}$$

$$6\frac{4}{5}$$
$$+\ 3\frac{2}{5}$$
$$\overline{9\frac{6}{5}} = 9 + 1\frac{1}{5} = 10\frac{1}{5}$$

Add. Write the answer in lowest terms.

1.
$$5\frac{1}{2}$$
$$+\ 4\frac{1}{2}$$
$$\overline{9\frac{2}{2}} =$$
$$9 + 1 = 10$$

2.
$$3\frac{1}{5}$$
$$+\ 2\frac{3}{5}$$

3.
$$2\frac{3}{8}$$
$$+\ 4\frac{1}{8}$$

4.
$$10\frac{4}{7}$$
$$+\ 8\frac{2}{7}$$

5.
$$6\frac{2}{6}$$
$$+\ 3\frac{5}{6}$$

6.
$$7\frac{8}{9}$$
$$+\ 8\frac{4}{9}$$

7.
$$27\frac{3}{10}$$
$$+\ 18\frac{6}{10}$$

8.
$$9\frac{3}{4}$$
$$+\ \ \frac{3}{4}$$

9.
$$17\frac{8}{15}$$
$$+\ 22\frac{9}{15}$$

10.
$$91\frac{7}{11}$$
$$+\ 8\frac{2}{11}$$

11.
$$3\frac{6}{100}$$
$$+\ 2\frac{39}{100}$$

12.
$$53\frac{16}{21}$$
$$+\ 46\frac{12}{21}$$

FRACTION IDEAS

9

Likes and Dislikes

Here's how to **add fractions** with **unlike denominators**.
First rewrite them with like denominators.

The least common denominator (LCD) is the smallest (nonzero) number that is a multiple of each of the two denominators.

$$\frac{1}{2} = \frac{3}{6}$$
$$+ \frac{1}{3} = \frac{2}{6}$$ LCD
$$\frac{5}{6}$$

$$\frac{2}{5} = \frac{4}{10}$$
$$+ \frac{1}{10} = \frac{1}{10}$$ LCD
$$\frac{5}{10} = \frac{1}{2}$$

$$\frac{5}{8} = \frac{15}{24}$$
$$+ \frac{5}{12} = \frac{10}{24}$$ LCD
$$\frac{25}{24} = 1\frac{1}{24}$$

Find the sums. Write each sum in lowest terms.

1.
$$\frac{1}{4} = \frac{3}{12}$$
$$+ \frac{1}{3} = \frac{4}{12}$$
$$\frac{7}{12}$$

2.
$$\frac{1}{2}$$
$$+ \frac{1}{8}$$

3.
$$\frac{1}{6}$$
$$+ \frac{3}{4}$$

4.
$$\frac{1}{3}$$
$$+ \frac{1}{6}$$

5.
$$\frac{3}{4}$$
$$+ \frac{1}{5}$$

6.
$$\frac{1}{18}$$
$$+ \frac{7}{9}$$

7.
$$\frac{7}{8}$$
$$+ \frac{5}{12}$$

8.
$$\frac{1}{4}$$
$$+ \frac{3}{20}$$

9.
$$\frac{2}{9}$$
$$+ \frac{3}{10}$$

10.
$$\frac{11}{24}$$
$$+ \frac{5}{12}$$

11.
$$\frac{4}{7}$$
$$+ \frac{1}{6}$$

12.
$$\frac{5}{6}$$
$$+ \frac{7}{10}$$

Skill: Adding fractions with unlike denominators

Unlike Anything I've Seen

Here's how to **add mixed numbers** with **unlike denominators**. Rewrite them with like denominators.

Use the least common denominator.

$$3\frac{2}{3} = 3\frac{4}{6}$$
$$+1\frac{5}{6} = 1\frac{5}{6}$$
$$4\frac{9}{6} = 4 + 1\frac{3}{6} = 5\frac{3}{6} = 5\frac{1}{2}$$

Find the sums. Write each sum in lowest terms.

1.
$$2\frac{1}{2} = 2\frac{5}{10}$$
$$+3\frac{2}{5} = 3\frac{4}{10}$$
$$5\frac{9}{10}$$

2.
$$8\frac{3}{4}$$
$$+7\frac{1}{12}$$

3.
$$4\frac{2}{3}$$
$$+3\frac{5}{6}$$

4.
$$9\frac{4}{11}$$
$$+8\frac{3}{10}$$

5.
$$5\frac{1}{2}$$
$$+4\frac{5}{6}$$

6.
$$16\frac{2}{5}$$
$$+5\frac{4}{9}$$

7.
$$23\frac{5}{8}$$
$$+16\frac{13}{16}$$

8.
$$5\frac{1}{3}$$
$$+8\frac{6}{7}$$

9.
$$7\frac{1}{10}$$
$$+6\frac{7}{30}$$

FRACTION IDEAS

Literary Lengths

Use what you know about adding fractions and mixed numbers to solve these problems.

Find the lowest common denominators.

Find the lowest common denominators.

1. Pinocchio's nose was $5\frac{7}{8}$ inches long before he told his first lie. It grew $2\frac{1}{4}$ inches when he lied. How long is his nose now? $8\frac{1}{8}$ $\quad 5\frac{7}{8} + 2\frac{2}{8} = 8\frac{1}{8}$

2. Rapunzel's hair was $2\frac{1}{7}$ feet long before she was locked in the tower. It grew $1\frac{3}{8}$ feet long in the tower. How long is her hair now? _____

3. Jack's beanstalk grew $5\frac{1}{2}$ feet the first week. Then in one day it grew $2\frac{3}{5}$ feet. How tall was the beanstalk then? _____

4. Cinderella danced for $1\frac{7}{8}$ hours before she met Prince Charming. She danced for $2\frac{1}{3}$ hours with him. How long did she dance? _____

5. Peter Pan flew for $3\frac{1}{2}$ hours alone. He flew with Wendy for $\frac{5}{6}$ hours. How long did he fly in all? _____

6. Little Red Riding Hood walked $\frac{3}{4}$ of a mile towards her grandmother's house before she rested. Then she walked $1\frac{1}{5}$ miles. How far did she walk in all? _____

FRACTION FACTS

Workout!

Test Your Skill

Find the sums. Give all answers in lowest terms.

1. $\dfrac{1}{8}$
$+ \dfrac{3}{8}$

2. $\dfrac{11}{16}$
$+ \dfrac{3}{16}$

3. $2\dfrac{1}{5}$
$+ \ \dfrac{3}{5}$

4. $7\dfrac{3}{10}$
$+ 5\dfrac{1}{10}$

5. $4\dfrac{2}{9} + 3\dfrac{4}{9} = $ _____

6. $10\dfrac{1}{8} + 3\dfrac{7}{8} = $ _____

7. $\dfrac{9}{10}$
$+ \dfrac{7}{10}$

8. $\dfrac{7}{16}$
$+ \dfrac{15}{16}$

9. $3\dfrac{7}{5}$
$+ 2\dfrac{5}{8}$

10. $2\dfrac{5}{12}$
$+ 5\dfrac{11}{12}$

11. $\dfrac{3}{4}$
$+ \dfrac{5}{8}$

12. $\dfrac{5}{6}$
$+ \dfrac{5}{12}$

13. $1\dfrac{2}{3}$
$+ 3\dfrac{1}{4}$

14. $2\dfrac{2}{5}$
$+ 3\dfrac{3}{10}$

15. $6\dfrac{1}{9} + 4\dfrac{1}{6} = $ _____

16. $7\dfrac{2}{3} + 3\dfrac{2}{9} = $ _____

Skill: Adding with fractions and mixed numbers

Same Old Leftovers

Here's how to **subtract fractions** with **like denominators.**
Subtract the numerators. Write the difference over the denominator.

Be sure to write your answer in lowest terms.

$$\frac{7}{8} - \frac{3}{8} = \frac{4}{8} = \frac{1}{2}$$

Find the differences. Give your answers in lowest terms.

1.
$$\frac{7}{9} - \frac{1}{9} = \frac{6}{9} = \frac{2}{3}$$

2.
$$\frac{4}{5} - \frac{2}{5} = \underline{\hspace{2cm}}$$

3.
$$\frac{2}{3} - \frac{1}{3} = \underline{\hspace{2cm}}$$

4.
$$\frac{3}{10} - \frac{1}{10} = \underline{\hspace{2cm}}$$

5.
$$\frac{6}{11} - \frac{4}{11} = \underline{\hspace{2cm}}$$

6.
$$\frac{17}{20} - \frac{10}{20} = \underline{\hspace{2cm}}$$

7.
$$\frac{6}{7} - \frac{3}{7} = \underline{\hspace{2cm}}$$

8.
$$\frac{3}{4} - \frac{1}{4} = \underline{\hspace{2cm}}$$

9.
$$\frac{7}{10} - \frac{3}{10} = \underline{\hspace{2cm}}$$

10.
$$\frac{11}{13} - \frac{8}{13} = \underline{\hspace{2cm}}$$

11.
$$\frac{33}{100} - \frac{8}{100} = \underline{\hspace{2cm}}$$

12.
$$\frac{10}{21} - \frac{10}{21} = \underline{\hspace{2cm}}$$

Skill: Subtracting fractions with like denominators

A Mixed Number by Any Other Name

Here's how to **subtract mixed numbers** with **like denominators.**
Sometimes you need to rename.

Rename $5\frac{1}{7}$ as $4\frac{8}{7}$.

$$5\frac{1}{7} = 4 + 1 + \frac{1}{7} = 4 + \frac{7}{7} + \frac{1}{7} = 4\frac{8}{7} \qquad \begin{array}{r} 4\frac{8}{7} \\ -2\frac{3}{7} \\ \hline 2\frac{5}{7} \end{array}$$

$$\begin{array}{r} 5\frac{1}{7} \\ -2\frac{3}{7} \\ \hline \end{array}$$

Subtract. Rename when necessary.

1. $\begin{array}{r} 8\frac{3}{7} = 7\frac{10}{7} \\ -5\frac{6}{7} = 5\frac{6}{7} \\ \hline 2\frac{4}{7} \end{array}$

2. $\begin{array}{r} 6 \\ -4\frac{1}{2} \\ \hline \end{array}$

3. $\begin{array}{r} 9\frac{9}{10} \\ -5\frac{3}{10} \\ \hline \end{array}$

4. $\begin{array}{r} 5\frac{3}{4} \\ -2\frac{1}{4} \\ \hline \end{array}$

5. $\begin{array}{r} 3 \\ -1\frac{2}{3} \\ \hline \end{array}$

6. $\begin{array}{r} 7\frac{5}{6} \\ -\frac{1}{6} \\ \hline \end{array}$

7. $\begin{array}{r} 4\frac{4}{5} \\ -3\frac{1}{5} \\ \hline \end{array}$

8. $\begin{array}{r} 12\frac{1}{4} \\ -8\frac{3}{4} \\ \hline \end{array}$

9. $\begin{array}{r} 15\frac{5}{12} \\ -10\frac{6}{12} \\ \hline \end{array}$

Skill: Subtracting mixed numbers with like denominators; renaming

A Lot Alike

Here's how to **subtract fractions** with **unlike denominators**.
First rewrite them with like denominators.

Use the least common denominator.

$$\dfrac{7}{9} = \dfrac{35}{45}$$
$$-\dfrac{2}{5} = \dfrac{18}{45}$$
$$\dfrac{17}{45}$$

$$\dfrac{5}{8} = \dfrac{10}{16}$$
$$-\dfrac{6}{16} = \dfrac{6}{16}$$
$$\dfrac{4}{16} = \dfrac{1}{4}$$

Find the differences. Write each difference in lowest terms.

1.
$$\dfrac{1}{2} = \dfrac{3}{6}$$
$$-\dfrac{1}{3} = \dfrac{2}{6}$$
$$\dfrac{1}{6}$$

2.
$$\dfrac{2}{3}$$
$$-\dfrac{1}{6}$$

3.
$$\dfrac{5}{6}$$
$$-\dfrac{1}{4}$$

4.
$$\dfrac{4}{5}$$
$$-\dfrac{3}{10}$$

5.
$$\dfrac{3}{4}$$
$$-\dfrac{5}{7}$$

6.
$$\dfrac{4}{6}$$
$$-\dfrac{4}{9}$$

7.
$$\dfrac{3}{4}$$
$$-\dfrac{1}{3}$$

8.
$$\dfrac{4}{7}$$
$$-\dfrac{5}{21}$$

9.
$$\dfrac{5}{8}$$
$$-\dfrac{1}{6}$$

Skill: Subtracting fractions with unlike denominators

A Different Mix

Here's how to **subtract mixed numbers** with **unlike denominators.** First rewrite them with like denominators.

Rename the mixed number if necessary.

$$5\frac{2}{3} = 5\frac{8}{12}$$
$$-3\frac{1}{4} = 3\frac{3}{12}$$
$$\overline{\phantom{-3\frac{1}{4}}} \quad 2\frac{5}{12}$$

$$6\frac{1}{4} = 6\frac{1}{4} = 5\frac{5}{4}$$
$$-2\frac{1}{2} = 2\frac{2}{4} = 2\frac{2}{4}$$
$$\overline{\phantom{-2\frac{1}{2}}} \quad 3\frac{3}{4}$$

Find the differences. Write each difference in lowest terms. Show your work.

1. $11\frac{5}{9} = \frac{10}{18}$
$-3\frac{1}{2} = \frac{9}{18}$
$\overline{}$ $8 \quad \frac{1}{18}$

2. $8\frac{3}{8}$
$-2\frac{3}{4}$

3. $9\frac{5}{6}$
$-8\frac{1}{4}$

4. $2\frac{1}{5}$
$-1\frac{7}{10}$

5. $11\frac{2}{3}$
$-3\frac{1}{2}$

6. $7\frac{5}{12}$
$-4\frac{7}{8}$

7. $6\frac{3}{4}$
$-\quad\frac{4}{5}$

8. 15
$-13\frac{5}{14}$

9. $23\frac{1}{10}$
$-20\frac{8}{15}$

Skill: Subtracting mixed numbers with unlike denominators

Fraction Frenzy

On the planet of Fractionia everyone's name begins with F, and no whole numbers or decimals are allowed, just fractions and mixed numbers.

Don't forget to reduce.

FLYING DISK

ICE CREAM

1. François found $6\frac{7}{15}$ footballs. He lost $1\frac{1}{2}$ footballs. How many does he have left? $4\frac{29}{30}$

2. Fred ate $3\frac{2}{5}$ pieces of fresh fruit. Frank ate $\frac{4}{7}$ pieces. How much more did Fred eat? _____

3. Fritz froze $9\frac{1}{2}$ yogurts. He ate $\frac{3}{4}$ of one for lunch. How many does he have left? _____

4. Fran framed $12\frac{1}{3}$ freshly painted pictures. Flo framed only $\frac{1}{5}$ picture. How many more pictures did Fran frame? _____

5. Frieda ate $6\frac{1}{8}$ French fries on Friday and $4\frac{3}{7}$ on Saturday. How many more did she eat on Friday? _____

6. Ferdie bought $7\frac{1}{3}$ Frisbees. Flo bought $9\frac{3}{7}$ Frisbees. How many more did Flo have? _____

7. Flora has $8\frac{2}{3}$ Fractionia dollars. Fiona has $6\frac{2}{5}$ Fractionia dollars. How much more does Flora have? _____

8. Fara had $2\frac{3}{8}$ Fractionia dollars. She spent $1\frac{5}{7}$ Fractionia dollars. How much does she have left? _____

Skill: Problem solving: Subtracting fractions and mixed numbers

Workout!

Test Your Skill

Find the differences. Write each difference in lowest terms.

1. $\dfrac{7}{8}$
$-\dfrac{3}{8}$

2. $\dfrac{9}{10}$
$-\dfrac{3}{10}$

3. $3\dfrac{7}{9}$
$-1\dfrac{2}{9}$

4. $5\dfrac{11}{12}$
$-2\dfrac{7}{12}$

5. $6\dfrac{4}{5} - 2\dfrac{3}{5} = $ _____

6. $7\dfrac{13}{16} - 3\dfrac{11}{16} = $ _____

7. $8\dfrac{1}{3}$
$-1\dfrac{2}{3}$

8. $4\dfrac{5}{9}$
$-\dfrac{8}{9}$

9. $7\dfrac{1}{10}$
$-3\dfrac{7}{10}$

10. $6\dfrac{5}{12}$
$-1\dfrac{11}{12}$

11. $\dfrac{4}{5}$
$-\dfrac{1}{3}$

12. $\dfrac{7}{10}$
$-\dfrac{1}{5}$

13. $4\dfrac{7}{8}$
$-2\dfrac{3}{4}$

14. $\dfrac{4}{9}$
$-\dfrac{1}{6}$

15. $\dfrac{2}{3} - \dfrac{1}{8} = $ _____

16. $4\dfrac{1}{3} - \dfrac{1}{5} = $ _____

17. $13\dfrac{7}{10}$
$-4\dfrac{5}{6}$

18. $6\dfrac{2}{3}$
$-4\dfrac{2}{3}$

19. $7\dfrac{1}{8}$
$-1\dfrac{3}{4}$

20. $4\dfrac{2}{7}$
$-3\dfrac{5}{8}$

PRACTICE TEST

Skill: Subtracting with fractions and mixed numbers

Multi-pliers

Here's how to **multiply fractions.** Multiply the numerators, then multiply the denominators.

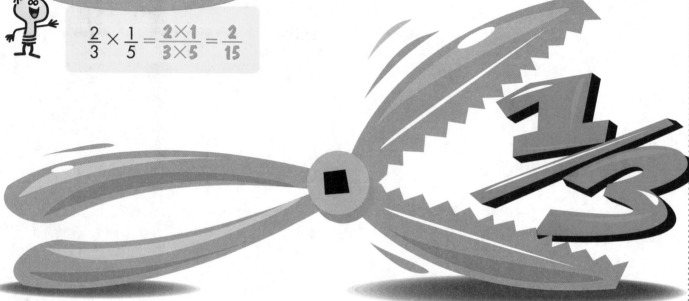

Just multiply straight across.

$$\frac{2}{3} \times \frac{1}{5} = \frac{2 \times 1}{3 \times 5} = \frac{2}{15}$$

Multiply. Give all answers in lowest terms.

1. $\frac{1}{2} \times \frac{2}{3} = \frac{2}{6} = \frac{1}{3}$

2. $\frac{2}{5} \times \frac{3}{7} =$ _____

3. $\frac{1}{3} \times \frac{1}{3} =$ _____

4. $\frac{3}{4} \times \frac{1}{2} =$ _____

5. $\frac{6}{7} \times \frac{10}{11} =$ _____

6. $\frac{1}{4} \times \frac{8}{9} =$ _____

7. $\frac{1}{2} \times \frac{1}{2} =$ _____

8. $\frac{1}{6} \times \frac{3}{4} =$ _____

9. $\frac{5}{8} \times \frac{1}{3} =$ _____

10. $\frac{3}{10} \times \frac{9}{20} =$ _____

11. $\frac{4}{5} \times \frac{5}{6} =$ _____

12. $\frac{7}{8} \times \frac{4}{7} =$ _____

Skill: Multiplying fractions

Camp Canceller

Here's how to **cancel** when you multiply. Reduce **before multiplying.** Use a slash and write what's left after dividing.

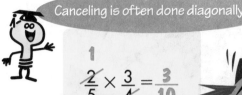

Canceling is often done diagonally.

$$\dfrac{\overset{1}{\cancel{2}}}{5} \times \dfrac{3}{\underset{2}{\cancel{4}}} = \dfrac{3}{10}$$

Find the products. Give answers in lowest terms.

1. $\dfrac{1}{2} \times \dfrac{4}{5}$

$$\dfrac{1}{\underset{1}{\cancel{2}}} \times \dfrac{\overset{2}{\cancel{4}}}{5} = \dfrac{2}{5}$$

2. $\dfrac{3}{4} \times \dfrac{8}{9}$

3. $\dfrac{1}{5} \times \dfrac{10}{13}$

4. $\dfrac{1}{8} \times \dfrac{16}{21}$

5. $\dfrac{12}{13} \times \dfrac{5}{18}$

6. $\dfrac{10}{21} \times \dfrac{3}{20}$

7. $\dfrac{1}{9} \times \dfrac{3}{8}$

8. $\dfrac{7}{12} \times \dfrac{6}{7}$

9. $\dfrac{15}{17} \times \dfrac{2}{3}$

10. $\dfrac{9}{10} \times \dfrac{3}{5}$

11. $\dfrac{17}{22} \times \dfrac{11}{34}$

12. $\dfrac{25}{36} \times \dfrac{18}{35}$

Skill: Multiplying with cancelling

Whole Ones

Here's how to **multiply fractions** and **whole numbers.**
Write the whole number as a fraction by putting it over 1.
Then multiply as you did with fractions.

Cancel if you can!
It makes your work easier!

$$\frac{1}{2} \times 6 = \frac{1}{\overset{}{\underset{1}{2}}} \times \frac{\overset{3}{\cancel{6}}}{1} = \frac{1}{1} \times \frac{3}{1} = \frac{3}{1} = 3$$

Find the products. Write answers in lowest terms.
Change any improper fraction answers to mixed numbers.

1. $\frac{1}{3} \times 5$

$\frac{1}{3} \times \frac{5}{1} = \frac{5}{3} = 1\frac{2}{3}$

2. $\frac{1}{2} \times 9$

3. $\frac{1}{5} \times 3$

4. $8 \times \frac{1}{4}$

5. $2 \times \frac{5}{7}$

6. $\frac{7}{10} \times 15$

7. $6 \times \frac{2}{3}$

8. $\frac{3}{4} \times 1$

9. $\frac{1}{8} \times 4$

10. $\frac{8}{13} \times 13$

11. $12 \times \frac{5}{9}$

12. $\frac{7}{8} \times 18$

FRACTION IDEAS

22

Improper Behavior

Here's how to **multiply mixed numbers.** Change them to improper fractions, then multiply. (Remember: When you change a mixed number to an improper fraction, you first multiply the whole number by the denominator, then add it to the numerator.)

Change back to a mixed number when you are done.

The problem: $2\frac{1}{3} \times \frac{1}{2}$

Step 1: Change to fractions

$2\frac{1}{3} = \frac{2\,(\times 3)}{1\,(\times 3)} + \frac{1}{3} = \frac{7}{3}$

Step 2: Multiply and reduce

$\frac{7}{3} \times \frac{1}{2} = \frac{7}{6} = 1\frac{1}{6}$

Find the products. Give answers in lowest terms.

1. $3\frac{2}{3} \times \frac{1}{6}$

$3\frac{2}{3} = \frac{11}{3}$

$\frac{11}{3} \times \frac{1}{6} = \frac{11}{18}$

2. $2\frac{1}{4} \times \frac{1}{3}$

3. $5\frac{5}{6} \times \frac{1}{7}$

4. $\frac{3}{4} \times 2\frac{2}{3}$

5. $\frac{5}{21} \times 4\frac{1}{5}$

6. $2\frac{1}{2} \times \frac{3}{10}$

7. $3\frac{1}{3} \times \frac{3}{10}$

8. $5 \times 1\frac{3}{5}$

9. $\frac{1}{18} \times 4\frac{1}{2}$

Skill: Multiplying mixed numbers

Glop for Everything

Use what you know about multiplying fractions and mixed numbers to solve the following problems. Show your work.

Give all answers in lowest terms.

1. The tiny-size bottle of X-L-ent Glop contains $\frac{4}{5}$ of a pint.
Directions say to use $\frac{1}{3}$ of a bottle to clean the bathtub.
How much Glop is that? $\frac{4}{15}$ pints $\frac{4}{5} \times \frac{1}{3} = \frac{4}{15}$

2. The regular-size bottle of X-L-ent Glop contains $\frac{3}{4}$ of a quart.
Directions say to use $\frac{2}{3}$ of a bottle to remove paint.
How much Glop is that? _____ quarts

3. The medium-size bottle of X-L-ent Glop contains $1\frac{1}{2}$ quarts.
Directions say to use $\frac{1}{6}$ of a bottle for turkey gravy.
How much Glop is that? _____ quarts

4. The large-size bottle of X-L-ent Glop contains 2 quarts.
Directions say to use $\frac{3}{8}$ of a bottle to polish shoes.
How much Glop is that? _____ quarts

5. The king-size bottle of X-L-ent Glop contains $2\frac{7}{8}$ quarts.
Directions say to use $\frac{4}{7}$ of a bottle to glue furniture.
How much Glop is that? _____ quarts

6. The huge-size bottle of X-L-ent Glop contains $1\frac{5}{7}$ gallons.
Directions say to use $3\frac{1}{2}$ bottles as skunk stench remover.
How much Glop is that? _____ gallons

FRACTION IDEAS

Skill: Problem solving: Multiplying fractions and mixed numbers

Find the products. Give answers in lowest terms.
Fill in the circle next to the correct answer.

1. $\frac{2}{9} \times \frac{1}{8}$ ○ $\frac{3}{9}$ ○ $\frac{3}{8}$
○ $7\frac{1}{8}$ ○ $\frac{1}{36}$

2. $\frac{1}{4} \times \frac{5}{6}$ ○ $\frac{5}{24}$ ○ $\frac{5}{4}$
○ $\frac{6}{4}$ ○ $\frac{4}{5}$

3. $\frac{5}{14} \times \frac{7}{10}$ ○ $\frac{1}{4}$ ○ $3\frac{1}{2}$
○ $\frac{57}{140}$ ○ $\frac{14}{30}$

4. $4 \times \frac{1}{5}$ ○ $\frac{4}{5}$ ○ $4\frac{1}{5}$
○ $5\frac{1}{4}$ ○ 20

5. $\frac{1}{3} \times 8$ ○ $8\frac{1}{3}$ ○ $3\frac{1}{8}$
○ $2\frac{2}{3}$ ○ $3\frac{1}{2}$

6. $5 \times \frac{3}{8}$ ○ $5\frac{3}{8}$ ○ $1\frac{7}{8}$
○ $3\frac{5}{8}$ ○ $5\frac{3}{5}$

7. $6 \times \frac{2}{3}$ ○ 12   ○ 4
○ 3   ○ 6

8. $1\frac{1}{8} \times 3\frac{1}{3}$ ○ $4\frac{5}{8}$ ○ $3\frac{3}{4}$
○ $3\frac{2}{8}$ ○ $3\frac{1}{4}$

9. $2\frac{5}{8} \times \frac{2}{3}$ ○ $1\frac{6}{8}$ ○ $1\frac{2}{3}$
○ $2\frac{1}{12}$ ○ $1\frac{3}{4}$

10. $4\frac{7}{12} \times 3\frac{3}{5}$ ○ $16\frac{1}{2}$ ○ $7\frac{11}{17}$
○ $7\frac{4}{12}$ ○ $17\frac{4}{5}$

PRACTICE TEST

Skill: Multiplying with fractions and mixed numbers

Flip It

To **divide a fraction** by another fraction, multiply
by the **reciprocal** of the second fraction.
To make the reciprocal, flip the fraction over.

Flip the fraction that comes after
the division sign. Then multiply.

reciprocals

$$\frac{1}{2} \div \frac{2}{3} = \frac{1}{2} \times \frac{3}{2} = \frac{3}{4}$$

Write the reciprocal of the divisor first. Then find the quotients.
Give answers in simplest form.

1. $\frac{3}{4} \div \frac{1}{3}$

$$\frac{3}{4} \times \frac{3}{1} = \frac{9}{4} = 2\frac{1}{4}$$

2. $\frac{1}{5} \div \frac{3}{5}$

3. $\frac{5}{6} \div \frac{5}{12}$

4. $\frac{1}{7} \div \frac{1}{8}$

5. $\frac{7}{10} \div \frac{1}{2}$

6. $\frac{8}{9} \div \frac{2}{3}$

7. $\frac{1}{12} \div \frac{3}{8}$

8. $\frac{5}{16} \div \frac{3}{4}$

9. $\frac{2}{3} \div \frac{2}{3}$

Skill: Dividing fractions

The Whole Thing Again

Here's how to **divide fractions** and **whole numbers**.
First, change the whole numbers to fractions. Then, multiply
by the reciprocal (flipover) of the divisor.

Remember, any whole number can
be written as itself over 1!

$$5 \div \frac{2}{3} = \frac{5}{1} \times \frac{3}{2} = \frac{15}{2} = 7\frac{1}{2}$$

$$\frac{3}{4} \div 2 = \frac{3}{4} \div \frac{2}{1} = \frac{3}{4} \times \frac{1}{2} = \frac{3}{8}$$

Find the quotients. Give answers in simplest form.

1. $2 \div \frac{1}{2}$

$$\frac{2}{1} \div \frac{1}{2} = \frac{2}{1} \times \frac{2}{1} = \mathbf{4}$$

2. $3 \div \frac{3}{4}$

3. $6 \div \frac{4}{5}$

4. $\frac{1}{2} \div 2$

5. $\frac{3}{4} \div 3$

6. $\frac{4}{5} \div 6$

7. $\frac{3}{8} \div 9$

8. $4 \div \frac{3}{4}$

9. $7 \div \frac{7}{8}$

10. $\frac{15}{16} \div \frac{3}{4}$

11. $1 \div \frac{9}{10}$

12. $\frac{25}{32} \div 50$

Skill: Dividing with whole numbers and fractions

Remixes

Here's how to **divide mixed numbers.** Change the mixed numbers to improper fractions and multiply by the reciprocal of the divisor.

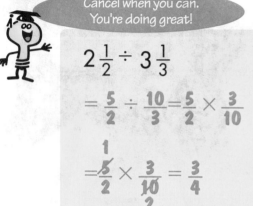

Cancel when you can. You're doing great!

$$2\frac{1}{2} \div 3\frac{1}{3}$$

$$= \frac{5}{2} \div \frac{10}{3} = \frac{5}{2} \times \frac{3}{10}$$

$$= \frac{\overset{1}{\cancel{5}}}{2} \times \frac{3}{\underset{2}{\cancel{10}}} = \frac{3}{4}$$

BAD BOYZ OF FRACTIONS

Find the quotients. Give answers in lowest form.

1. $2\frac{1}{4} \div \frac{2}{3}$

$$\frac{9}{4} \div \frac{2}{3} = \frac{9}{4} \times \frac{3}{2} = \frac{27}{8} = 3\frac{3}{8}$$

2. $\frac{4}{5} \div 1\frac{1}{3}$

3. $4\frac{1}{2} \div \frac{3}{4}$

4. $1\frac{3}{4} \div \frac{7}{8}$

5. $3\frac{1}{2} \div 1\frac{1}{2}$

6. $5\frac{1}{3} \div 5\frac{1}{3}$

7. $3\frac{3}{4} \div 2\frac{1}{2}$

8. $2\frac{2}{5} \div 1\frac{1}{5}$

9. $6\frac{1}{8} \div 4\frac{2}{3}$

10. $2\frac{1}{3} \div \frac{1}{100}$

11. $\frac{1}{8} \div 10\frac{1}{4}$

12. $12\frac{2}{3} \div 3\frac{1}{6}$

Serve it Yourself!

There are 12 ounces in every package of Bing. Use what you know to find how many of each size serving there are in a package of Bing.

When you divide by a fraction, remember to invert.

Divide fractions and whole numbers to find the answers.

1. One serving $\frac{1}{4}$ ounce.

How many servings in the whole package? __48__ $12 \div \frac{1}{4} = \frac{12}{1} \times \frac{4}{1} = 48$

2. One serving $= \frac{1}{3}$ ounce.

How many servings in the whole package? _____

3. One serving $= 2$ ounces.

How many servings in the whole package? _____

4. One serving $= 1\frac{4}{5}$ ounces.

How many servings in the whole package? _____

5. One serving $= 2\frac{1}{2}$ ounces.

How many servings in the whole package? _____

6. One serving $= 3\frac{3}{7}$ ounces.

How many servings in the whole package? _____

Skill: Problem solving: Dividing with fractions and mixed numbers

Workout!

Test Your Skill

Find each answer. Give answers in lowest terms.
Fill in the circle next to the correct answer.

1. $\frac{1}{6} \div \frac{1}{4}$
   ◯ 24   ◯ $\frac{4}{6}$
   ◯ $\frac{11}{2}$ ◯ $\frac{2}{3}$

2. $\frac{2}{3} \div \frac{3}{4}$
   ◯ 2   ◯ $\frac{1}{2}$
   ◯ $\frac{8}{9}$ ◯ $\frac{9}{8}$

3. $8 \div \frac{1}{3}$
   ◯ $\frac{3}{8}$ ◯ $2\frac{2}{3}$
   ◯ 24   ◯ $\frac{2}{3}$

4. $\frac{4}{5} \div 9$
   ◯ $\frac{44}{5}$ ◯ $\frac{9}{5}$
   ◯ $9\frac{4}{5}$ ◯ $\frac{4}{45}$

5. $\frac{5}{6} \div \frac{2}{3}$
   ◯ $\frac{3}{20}$ ◯ $1\frac{1}{4}$
   ◯ $\frac{5}{9}$ ◯ $1\frac{1}{12}$

6. $1\frac{7}{8} \div \frac{3}{5}$
   ◯ $3\frac{1}{8}$ ◯ $\frac{17}{13}$
   ◯ $\frac{11}{75}$ ◯ $\frac{13}{20}$

7. $2\frac{1}{2} \div \frac{3}{8}$
   ◯ $\frac{3}{20}$ ◯ $6\frac{2}{3}$
   ◯ $1\frac{15}{16}$ ◯ $\frac{15}{16}$

8. $3\frac{3}{8} \div \frac{3}{4}$
   ◯ $5\frac{1}{6}$ ◯ $2\frac{29}{32}$
   ◯ $4\frac{1}{2}$ ◯ $\frac{6}{31}$

9. $2\frac{1}{7} \div 3\frac{4}{7}$
   ◯ $7\frac{33}{56}$ ◯ $1\frac{19}{160}$
   ◯ $\frac{64}{49}$ ◯ $\frac{3}{5}$

10. $3\frac{5}{9} \div 1\frac{3}{5}$
   ◯ $\frac{20}{29}$ ◯ $5\frac{31}{45}$
   ◯ $2\frac{2}{9}$ ◯ $\frac{9}{20}$

Skill: Dividing with fractions and mixed numbers

Answer Key

Page 1 **1.** $\frac{1}{4}$; **2.** $\frac{5}{8}$; **3.** $\frac{7}{16}$; **4.** $\frac{2}{3}$; **5.** $\frac{1}{6}$; **6.** $\frac{3}{4}$; **7.** $\frac{4}{4}$; **8.** $\frac{2}{9}$; **9.** ⊘ or ▦

Page 2 **1.** $7\frac{1}{3}$; **2.** $5\frac{3}{8}$; **3.** $3\frac{1}{4}$; **4.** $8\frac{2}{5}$; **5.** $4\frac{1}{2}$; **6.** ■ ■ ■ ■ ▤

Page 3 **1.** $\frac{1}{2}$ jar; **2.** $\frac{15}{18}$ gallon; **3.** $\frac{16}{20}$ loaf; **4.** $\frac{1}{3}$ bag; **5.** $\frac{3}{4}$ pie; **6.** $\frac{6}{16}$ cup

Page 4 **1.** $\frac{2}{3}$; **2.** $\frac{3}{5}$; **3.** $\frac{1}{3}$; **4.** $\frac{1}{4}$; **5.** $\frac{1}{2}$; **6.** $\frac{2}{3}$; **7.** $\frac{2}{5}$; **8.** $\frac{1}{5}$; **9.** $\frac{2}{5}$; **10.** $\frac{1}{4}$; **11.** $\frac{2}{3}$; **12.** $\frac{3}{4}$

Page 5 (From left to right) **1.** $1\frac{1}{2}$; **2.** 1; **3.** $1\frac{3}{4}$; **4.** $1\frac{1}{10}$; **5.** $5\frac{1}{3}$; **6.** 3; **7.** $2\frac{1}{8}$; **8.** $9\frac{1}{6}$; **9.** $3\frac{1}{2}$; **10.** 4; **11.** 4; **12.** $1\frac{4}{5}$; **13.** $5\frac{2}{7}$; **14.** $2\frac{1}{5}$; **15.** 7

Page 6 **1.** They drank the same; **2.** They ate the same; they both reduce to $\frac{1}{2}$; **3.** Both are right; $\frac{9}{12}$ reduces to $\frac{3}{4}$; **4.** 20; **5.** Rudy's ($\frac{20}{2}=10$ inches); **6.** Glenn had $\frac{1}{6}$ dozen more.

Page 7 **1.** $\frac{2}{7}$; **2.** $2\frac{3}{8}$; **3.** $\frac{4}{8}$ or $\frac{1}{2}$; **4.** $1\frac{2}{5}$; **5.** $\frac{2}{4}, \frac{3}{6}, \frac{4}{8}$; answers will vary; **6.** $\frac{2}{3}, \frac{4}{6}, \frac{6}{9}$; answers will vary; **7.** $\frac{1}{4}$; **8.** $\frac{3}{4}$; **9.** $\frac{1}{3}$; **10.** 4; **11.** $5\frac{1}{3}$; **12.** $\frac{1}{3}$; **13.** $1\frac{1}{3}$; **14.** $\frac{2}{3}$; **15.** 5; **16.** $4\frac{1}{4}$; **17.** $\frac{3}{4}$; **18.** $1\frac{2}{3}$

Page 8 **1.** $\frac{1}{2}$; **2.** $\frac{5}{7}$; **3.** $\frac{2}{3}$; **4.** $\frac{4}{5}$; **5.** 1; **6.** $1\frac{2}{5}$; **7.** $1\frac{2}{3}$; **8.** $1\frac{1}{6}$; **9.** $\frac{5}{6}$; **10.** 1

Page 9 **1.** 10; **2.** $5\frac{4}{5}$; **3.** $6\frac{1}{2}$; **4.** $18\frac{6}{7}$; **5.** $10\frac{1}{6}$; **6.** $16\frac{1}{3}$; **7.** $45\frac{9}{10}$; **8.** $10\frac{1}{2}$; **9.** $40\frac{2}{15}$; **10.** $99\frac{9}{11}$; **11.** $5\frac{9}{20}$; **12.** $100\frac{1}{3}$

Page 10 **1.** $\frac{7}{12}$; **2.** $\frac{5}{8}$; **3.** $\frac{11}{12}$; **4.** $\frac{1}{2}$; **5.** $\frac{19}{20}$; **6.** $\frac{5}{6}$; **7.** $1\frac{7}{24}$; **8.** $\frac{2}{5}$; **9.** $\frac{47}{90}$; **10.** $\frac{7}{8}$; **11.** $\frac{31}{42}$; **12.** $1\frac{8}{15}$

Page 11 **1.** $5\frac{9}{10}$; **2.** $15\frac{5}{6}$; **3.** $8\frac{1}{2}$; **4.** $17\frac{73}{110}$; **5.** $10\frac{1}{3}$; **6.** $21\frac{38}{45}$; **7.** $40\frac{7}{16}$; **8.** $14\frac{4}{21}$; **9.** $13\frac{1}{3}$

Page 12 **1.** $8\frac{1}{8}$ in.; **2.** $3\frac{29}{56}$ ft; **3.** $8\frac{1}{10}$ ft; **4.** $4\frac{5}{24}$ hr; **5.** $4\frac{1}{3}$ hr; **6.** $1\frac{19}{20}$ mi

Page 13 **1.** $\frac{1}{2}$; **2.** $\frac{7}{8}$; **3.** $2\frac{4}{5}$; **4.** $12\frac{2}{5}$; **5.** $7\frac{2}{3}$; **6.** 14; **7.** $1\frac{3}{5}$; **8.** $1\frac{3}{8}$; **9.** $7\frac{1}{40}$; **10.** $8\frac{1}{3}$; **11.** $1\frac{3}{8}$; **12.** $1\frac{1}{4}$; **13.** $4\frac{11}{12}$; **14.** $5\frac{7}{10}$; **15.** $10\frac{5}{18}$; **16.** $10\frac{8}{9}$

Page 14 **1.** $\frac{2}{3}$; **2.** $\frac{2}{5}$; **3.** $\frac{1}{3}$; **4.** $\frac{1}{5}$; **5.** $\frac{2}{11}$; **6.** $\frac{7}{20}$; **7.** $\frac{3}{7}$; **8.** $\frac{1}{2}$; **9.** $\frac{2}{5}$; **10.** $\frac{3}{13}$; **11.** $\frac{1}{4}$; **12.** 0

Page 15 **1.** $2\frac{4}{7}$; **2.** $1\frac{1}{2}$; **3.** $4\frac{3}{5}$; **4.** $3\frac{1}{2}$; **5.** $1\frac{1}{3}$; **6.** $7\frac{2}{3}$; **7.** $1\frac{3}{5}$; **8.** $3\frac{1}{2}$; **9.** $4\frac{11}{12}$

Answer Key

2. $\frac{1}{2}$; **3.** $\frac{7}{12}$; **4.** $\frac{1}{2}$; **5.** $\frac{1}{28}$; **6.** $\frac{2}{9}$; **7.** $\frac{5}{12}$; **8.** $\frac{1}{3}$; **9.** $\frac{11}{24}$

$8\frac{1}{18}$; **2.** $5\frac{5}{8}$; **3.** $1\frac{7}{12}$; **4.** $\frac{1}{2}$; **5.** $8\frac{1}{6}$; **6.** $2\frac{13}{24}$; **7.** $5\frac{19}{20}$; **8.** $1\frac{9}{14}$; **9.** $2\frac{17}{30}$

1. $4\frac{29}{30}$ left; **2.** $2\frac{29}{35}$ more; **3.** $8\frac{3}{4}$ left; **4.** $12\frac{2}{15}$ more; **5.** $1\frac{39}{56}$ more; **6.** $2\frac{2}{21}$ more; **7.** $2\frac{4}{15}$ more;

19 1. $\frac{1}{2}$; **2.** $\frac{3}{5}$; **3.** $2\frac{5}{9}$; **4.** $3\frac{1}{3}$; **5.** $4\frac{1}{5}$; **6.** $4\frac{1}{8}$; **7.** $6\frac{2}{3}$; **8.** $3\frac{2}{3}$; **9.** $3\frac{2}{5}$; **10.** $4\frac{1}{2}$; **11.** $\frac{7}{15}$; **12.** $\frac{1}{2}$;

. $2\frac{1}{8}$; **14.** $\frac{5}{18}$; **15.** $\frac{13}{24}$; **16.** $4\frac{2}{15}$; **17.** $8\frac{13}{15}$; **18.** 2; **19.** $5\frac{3}{8}$; **20.** $\frac{37}{56}$

Page 20 1. $\frac{1}{3}$; **2.** $\frac{6}{35}$; **3.** $\frac{1}{9}$; **4.** $\frac{3}{8}$; **5.** $\frac{60}{77}$; **6.** $\frac{2}{9}$; **7.** $\frac{1}{4}$; **8.** $\frac{1}{8}$; **9.** $\frac{5}{24}$; **10.** $\frac{27}{200}$; **11.** $\frac{2}{3}$; **12.** $\frac{1}{2}$

Page 21 1. $\frac{2}{5}$; **2.** $\frac{2}{3}$; **3.** $\frac{2}{13}$; **4.** $\frac{2}{21}$; **5.** $\frac{10}{39}$; **6.** $\frac{1}{14}$; **7.** $\frac{1}{24}$; **8.** $\frac{1}{2}$; **9.** $\frac{10}{17}$; **10.** $\frac{27}{50}$; **11.** $\frac{1}{4}$; **12.** $\frac{5}{14}$

Page 22 1. $1\frac{2}{3}$; **2.** $4\frac{1}{2}$; **3.** $\frac{3}{5}$; **4.** 2; **5.** $1\frac{3}{7}$; **6.** $10\frac{1}{2}$; **7.** 4; **8.** $\frac{3}{4}$; **9.** $\frac{1}{2}$; **10.** 8; **11.** $6\frac{2}{3}$; **12.** $15\frac{3}{4}$

Page 23 1. $\frac{11}{18}$; **2.** $\frac{3}{4}$; **3.** $\frac{5}{6}$; **4.** 2; **5.** 1; **6.** $\frac{3}{4}$; **7.** 1; **8.** 8; **9.** $\frac{1}{4}$

Page 24 1. $\frac{4}{15}$; **2.** $\frac{1}{2}$ qt. or 1 pt.; **3.** $\frac{1}{4}$; **4.** $\frac{3}{4}$; **5.** $1\frac{9}{14}$; **6.** 6

Page 25 1. $\frac{1}{36}$; **2.** $\frac{5}{24}$; **3.** $\frac{1}{4}$; **4.** $\frac{4}{5}$; **5.** $2\frac{2}{3}$; **6.** $1\frac{7}{8}$; **7.** 4; **8.** $3\frac{3}{4}$; **9.** $1\frac{3}{4}$; **10.** $16\frac{1}{2}$

Page 26 1. $2\frac{1}{4}$; **2.** $\frac{1}{3}$; **3.** 2; **4.** $1\frac{1}{7}$; **5.** $1\frac{2}{5}$; **6.** $1\frac{1}{3}$; **7.** $\frac{2}{9}$; **8.** $\frac{5}{12}$; **9.** 1

Page 27 1. 4; **2.** 4; **3.** $7\frac{1}{2}$; **4.** $\frac{1}{4}$; **5.** $\frac{1}{4}$; **6.** $\frac{2}{15}$; **7.** $\frac{1}{24}$; **8.** $5\frac{1}{3}$; **9.** 8; **10.** $1\frac{1}{4}$; **11.** $1\frac{1}{9}$; **12.** $\frac{1}{64}$

Page 28 1. $3\frac{3}{8}$; **2.** $\frac{3}{5}$; **3.** 6; **4.** 2; **5.** $2\frac{1}{3}$; **6.** 1; **7.** $1\frac{1}{2}$; **8.** 2; **9.** $1\frac{5}{16}$; **10.** $233\frac{1}{3}$; **11.** $\frac{1}{82}$; **12.** 4

Page 29 1. 48; **2.** 36; **3.** 6; **4.** $6\frac{2}{3}$; **5.** $4\frac{4}{5}$; **6.** $3\frac{1}{2}$

Page 30 1. $\frac{2}{3}$; **2.** $\frac{8}{9}$; **3.** 24; **4.** $\frac{4}{45}$; **5.** $1\frac{1}{4}$; **6.** $3\frac{1}{8}$; **7.** $6\frac{2}{3}$; **8.** $4\frac{1}{2}$; **9.** $\frac{3}{5}$; **10.** $2\frac{2}{9}$